Leading with Style

The Comprehensive Guide to Leadership Styles

Jonathan Sandling

Introduction

In many ways leadership is a simple concept: leaders aim to inspire, enthuse and motivate others in the achievement of a common goal. But when you consider the diversity of leader personalities, their staff and the professions in which they operate the subject of leadership begins to grow in complexity. Most leaders know what they should be doing, but for some reason they just don't do it. Within leadership there is an urgent need to make common sense, common practice, and this book will undoubtedly support the leader as they strive to develop the necessary skills and knowledge that are required for success.

This book will identify a range of leadership styles which can be adopted by leaders in order to meet the specific requirements of different situations. It must be stressed from the outset that there is no right or wrong leadership style but rather the styles explored within this book should be viewed in accordance to the situation that presents itself.

There is a main focus around leadership within the workplace however the concepts covered within this book can be applied to any other leadership situation. When the book refers to 'staff' or 'employees' it can also be regarded as being relevant to leading friends, athletes, communities or any other group of individuals. If you are reading this book from a non-work related point of view you are advised to transfer the ideas and examples that are presented and use them in a way that relates to your own specific situation.

It is unfortunately beyond the scope of this book to cover every single leadership style and every single variation of style that exists however eight of the most commonly discussed leadership styles have been selected for presentation. The eight distinct leadership styles contained within this book provide a thorough introduction and well-rounded exploration of the topic.

The initial chapter begins by looking at leadership in general terms in order to establish a starting point on which to build upon. The chapters that follow go on to explore eight different leadership styles in isolation. Each of these chapters will be structured using the same sub-sections: introduction; key strengths; key criticisms; and final thoughts. This consistent chapter structure has been adopted as it allows for easy comparison between styles for the reader. Once the eight leadership styles have been presented the closing chapters will further the subject by discussing the varying relationships that exist between different leadership style pairs.

The book will come to a close by presenting a number of other leadership style theories and concepts. The eight distinct styles covered throughout the core of this book provide a sufficient overview of the topic of leadership styles however it is important to also consider some additional thoughts and ideas on the subject. This will also ensure that you are familiar with a broader range of leadership terms and concepts.

Chapters

What is Leadership?

The initial chapter of this book has been dedicated to the topic of leadership. It is essential that a sound understanding of leadership is established prior to exploring leadership styles. Leadership is the skill that needs to be performed and the leadership style is the way in which to perform it. You can't discuss football tactics in any great depth if you do not know how to play the game in the first place.

Leadership Definitions

An obvious place to start is with a small selection of leadership definitions. Some of the most commonly used definitions of leadership have been presented below.

"The only definition of a leader is someone who has followers" – Peter Drucker

"Leadership is the ability to turn vision into reality" – Warren Bennis

"Leaders are those who empower others" – Bill Gates

"Leadership is influence – nothing more, nothing less" - John Maxwell

These definitions are fine, and they do identify some fundamental principles of leadership, however they are lacking in some critical areas. Simply having followers does not necessarily make you a leader, turning vision into reality can be achieved in the absence of leadership, empowering others is great but it lacks direction and influencing people implies leadership is about authority and power which it most certainly is not.

Below is my own definition which I believe provides a slightly more comprehensive outline of what leadership is. Ultimately it brings together key points from the definitions presented above as well as some additional points which are absent.

"Leadership is a process of social engagement, which inspires and maximises the efforts of others, towards the achievement of a common goal"

Leadership evolves from social engagement rather than from the authority and power of the individual leader. Leaders need other people more than anything else and by inspiring and maximising the efforts of others the leader will be more effective in achieving their desired goal. The focus on the goal is also of vital importance as leaders need to provide clear direction and clarity to their followers. Making it a common goal is essential as agreement and belief in the vision needs to come from everyone involved and should not just be enforced by the leader.

Any definition of leadership could be challenged but as long as the core principles of inspiring and supporting others in the achievement of a common goal are incorporated little significant argument can be justified against it.

Leadership in Context

Definitions are very useful but they fail to put leadership into context. Leadership is all about inspiring other people, motivating them to take action and providing them with direction and clarity. It is about energising people, building self-belief in them and supporting them to achieve their goals. Effective leaders understand that they need other people in order to succeed. They know they need to support these people and guide them as they strive to achieve their objectives. Good leaders understand their staff, believe in them and support them in any way they can. They will also have a high level of emotional intelligence which is used to build meaningful working relationships with others. Leadership is about relationships and collaboration, not power and status.

Leadership is Over-Emphasised

Leadership is often considered to be something to strive for – as though only a select few people are capable of achieving the title of 'leader'. But this is simply not true. Everyone can be a leader in one way or another. Think about a time when someone has supported you, provided you with direction and inspired you to take action. You may be thinking of an old boss you had or a family member. Your parents may have led you through your school years, guided you, supported you and motivated you to achieve and succeed. You may not class your parents as leaders but they definitely are.

Similarly, you may have been inspired by a famous celebrity who has opened your eyes to the possibility of achieving greatness. This celebrity has been a leader to you even though you have never met them. And what about those throw-away comments you hear on the bus or at work which have had a lasting effect on you? You may have heard somebody say something many years ago which has always stuck in your mind. Words which you refer to when you are feeling low and you need to motivate yourself. These people have been leaders to you even though you may have only exchanged conversation with them on a few occasions or perhaps even just over heard them speaking to someone else.

Leadership Comes in Many Forms

Leadership comes in many forms and it is not just about changing the world with large sweeping ideological movements. Leadership is about meaningful interaction between two or more people, where one or both parties are enthused and inspired as a consequence. How this interaction occurs is generally irrelevant, it is the outcome of the interaction that is of the upmost importance.

Therefore, as each leadership style is explored over the following chapters it is important to remember that the style being used is nothing more than a 'style'. Regardless of the leadership style being used it is essential to always refer back to the fundamental principles of leadership which have been outlined within this chapter.

No leadership style should be regarded as being either good or bad and none are ideal in every situation. They all have their place depending on when, where and how they are being used. Leadership styles enable leaders to be flexible, adaptable and diverse in their actions. Leadership styles are a fundamental component of leadership and it is for this reason that this book has been dedicated to this topic.

Autocratic Leadership

Autocratic Leadership is sometimes referred to as the 'classic' or 'traditional' approach to leadership. It involves the leader retaining all the power and leading by instruction. Employees will have little or no input in any decision making processes and will work completely under the direction of the leader. When you think of this style of leadership it often conjures up images of the old-fashioned hard-nosed boss. Military leaders are commonly found to adopt this style of leadership in their aim to control and command their troops.

An autocratic leader will tell people what to do rather than ask them. They will create the goals, set the targets, assign the job roles and drive performance. The employees will have little or no say in how they conduct their work or what it is they are aiming to achieve. Autocratic leadership is often used when dealing with people who have a low level of knowledge and experience. It is also used in situations when decisions need to be made in a short time frame.

Many people view autocratic leadership as being an out-dated style of leadership. In the past a vast number of managers and leaders considered the direct nature of autocratic leadership to be the only way to get people to do what they wanted. You had to be tough and firm with people or they would take liberties. However, in the modern world of business where the values, feelings and opinions of the employees are more regularly considered, this style of leadership is implemented less frequently. Even though many leaders would frown upon the use of an autocratic style, as we progress through this chapter it will become clear that it still has a valid place in the overall leadership armoury of modern leaders.

It is important to understand that a leader does not simply pick a leadership style and use it regardless of the situation. Instead they will jump from one style to another throughout a period time and for some situations autocratic leadership may be the most suitable option. In addition, autocratic leadership must not be confused with rudeness and insensitivity. Just because a leader is being assertive and instructional in their leadership style does not necessarily mean they are being rude and disrespectful.

I have heard many leadership professionals advising that autocratic leadership should not be used in the modern world of business. This is a ridiculous notion as you will hopefully see. I completely agree that this style of leadership should only be used when absolutely necessary but in some situations it is definitely required. I am not suggesting leaders should go around all day barking orders at people but in some cases the leader will need to be autocratic and they will not be leading effectively if they do not have this style of leadership at their disposal.

Key Strengths

Some situations and work environments require an autocratic approach in order to ensure work is completed effectively, on time and in a safe manner. Employees sometimes need clarity regarding what is expected of them. When someone lacks the basic understanding of the bigger picture they often need a leader to simply tell them what they need to do. This can actually indirectly motivate and engage people as the provision of a clear objective is sometimes all it takes. This can be the case for employees who are new to a job role or those who have a low level of skill and experience.

Autocratic leadership is often witnessed when a leader is dealing with employees who have very low levels of knowledge, experience and skill. When this is coupled with insufficient time to train and educate the staff member a more direct approach to leadership is required in order to complete tasks within predetermined timescales. Obviously it is important to adopt an alternative leadership style when sufficient time becomes available to train and educate the employee but when deadlines are tight, and tasks need to be completed on-time, being autocratic is often the best option for both the leader and the employee.

Another key strength of autocratic leadership is that it is often required in order to maintain the welfare of the staff. Due to having greater knowledge and experience the leader is sometimes the only person who has the understanding and foresight to see that the employees are placing themselves at risk. If this is the case it is the leader's responsibility to provide clear and direct instruction to ensure their safety.

For example, if an employee is using a piece of machinery incorrectly, placing themselves and their colleagues at risk, the leader has a duty of care to step in and deal with the situation in an autocratic style. As previously stated this does not mean the leader has to be rude and aggressive but they do have to be assertive and clear in their instruction. This can be followed up with appropriate training and support to prevent the situation from occurring again. This example highlights the need for autocratic leadership in certain situations and also highlights that this style of leadership is not detached from values and support of staff as staff welfare and safety is paramount in this case.

Key Criticisms

The biggest criticism for autocratic leadership is that it is too prescriptive and it does not consider and incorporate the opinions and expertise of the employees. This in turn results in a lack of opportunity for development within the workforce. Poorly skilled staff will always be poorly skilled if all the leader does is tell them what to do, never allowing them to think for themselves and explore new ideas.

If the employees are never exposed to decision making processes or never have the opportunity to think for themselves their development will be minimised. They will always learn by doing, but once they have mastered the job they have been given there is no scope or opportunity to develop beyond that point. Without engaging and working with employees they will never be able to flourish and reach their potential.

Predominant and consistent use of autocratic leadership has been linked to high staff turnover, poor morale, lack of development and lack of respect for the leader. Staff will demonstrate decreased levels of motivation and will be uninspired to work. Innovation and creativity will be limited and staff will feel undervalued and unappreciated as individuals. Although autocratic leadership can be justified in certain situations it should never be used as a primary leadership style as it is far too inhibiting for employees.

Final Thoughts

Many modern perspectives of autocratic leadership look at it as an out-dated and irrelevant leadership style. Although leading with a values-based approach is highly admirable it is simply not realistic in every situation. Autocratic leadership still has a place in the modern business however it just needs to be used in an appropriate way. It can also be argued that autocratic leadership indirectly provides value and support for staff as it can contribute towards achievement, safety and job security.

It must be stressed once again that autocratic leadership should not be a leader's preferred style as it does not empower staff, nor does it provide them with opportunities for development. But its relevance in some situations, particularly where staff safety and pressure to achieve short-term targets is concerned, should not be overlooked. As long as autocratic leadership is combined with more supportive leadership styles it will remain to be a fundamental element of effective leadership.

Democratic Leadership

Democratic leaders focus on the needs, opinions and values of their employees. They listen to their ideas, empathise with their beliefs and actively seek their input. This style of leadership empowers staff and places them at the centre of the decision making process. It is often considered as being a polar opposite to autocratic leadership. As with all leadership styles there is a time and place for democratic leadership and effective leaders know when to use it and when not to use it.

If you live in the western world you will be part of a democratic society. This means that you will live freely within a structured environment. Governments provide structure by establishing laws and rules but within these constraints people are able to live freely. A democratic leader will create their own democracy within the workplace. They will outline the rules, which will incorporate the views of the staff, and the staff will work freely within that environment.

When making decisions that impact the whole team a democratic leader will ensure they obtain the views of the employees before committing to any actions. For example, if the leader is establishing organisational objectives, rather than setting them independently, the leader will include the employees in the process. Employee input will ensure that the views and opinions of the staff have been incorporated and with everyone contributing to the objectives there will be a feeling of collective ownership.

The input of employees is vital for effective democratic leadership but it must be noted that the final decision still lies with the leader. In democratic leadership either the leader must make the decision or if the decision has been made by the staff the leader must approve it. Good democratic leaders are able to make calculated decisions based on the valuable input from their staff. Some information provided will be highly relevant and some will be highly irrelevant. The leader must consider everything that is presented and make an informed decision using their own unique knowledge and experience.

Key Strengths

Democratic leadership encourages the creation of common or collective goals. It enables both leaders and employees to devise and agree upon a course of action or vision for the future. If the leader involves their staff in the decision making process the final decision will be a collective agreement. It will be just as much a staff decision to pursue a course of action as it is a leadership decision. This collective responsibility and agreement on the actions that are to be taken can result in greater adherence to the task on the part of the employees. In turn, employees will demonstrate higher levels of engagement, enthusiasm and motivation to perform. Rather than being told what to do in an autocratic style, staff will have the opportunity to decide for themselves.

Effective leaders understand that they need other people in order to be successful. Leaders need people because they are often more knowledgeable and experienced than they are in many different areas. A well educated and vastly experienced marketing manager will typically be able to provide more effective marketing strategies than a less knowledgeable leader. Similarly, they will be able to evaluate and provide informed advantages and disadvantages for any ideas the leader may come up with. Being democratic allows such staff to flourish and contribute for the greater benefit of the organisation.

Even if the leader is dealing with an employee who has a low level of skill they can still be democratic. Whereas, previously it was proposed that autocratic leadership may be suitable in this situation, being democratic can also have its benefits. It may not be appropriate to request advanced analytical data from this member of staff but there are many other ways in which to involve them in decision making and planning. Involvement and freedom around when they take their breaks, how they manage their day, who they want to work with and what skills they would like to develop in the future can be discussed at any level of employment. Sometimes the simple things can make the biggest difference and encouraging staff input into these areas can significantly enhance performance and engagement.

Key Criticisms

Involving employees in the decision making process can sometimes confuse matters unnecessarily. Too many opinions and ideas can overcomplicate things and make the decision making process complex and time consuming when it need not be. Some situations and issues are better dealt with in a different way with the leader taking decisive action. Often the decision is a simple one and the leader does not need to consult his employees but rather deal with it independently.

If the leader is in a position where they are leading staff who have low levels of skills, experience and knowledge a democratic approach to leadership may not be suitable in every case. It could still be used in personal situations, such as agreeing on development opportunities or establishing improved employee work patterns, but when the leader is faced with a complex situation the input of a low level staff member may not be of significant benefit.

It is all about matching the right person with the right task and engaging them in an effective way. If the wrong person is matched to the wrong task then a democratic style can be disastrous. This is where the structure and constraints of a democracy play an important role. If the leader can establish an appropriate structure in which their staff can work freely and effectively then democratic leadership can work extremely well. However, when is goes wrong the issue is usually associated with the leader's inability to establish a sufficient structure for the staff to effectively operate within.

Final Thoughts

Democratic leadership is sometimes discussed as being a good way of getting the staff to 'feel' involved and a good way of ensuring staff 'believe' they have been listened to. However, this is an extremely patronising and arrogant view as the leader should not request input from their staff just to make them 'feel' included but rather the leader should 'want' to include the staff as great benefit can be gained from their input. True democratic leaders listen to their staff, value their opinions and incorporate their input into their decisions and planning.

Many employees will have greater knowledge and experience than the leader and a good leader will tap into this resource as frequently as possible. An effective leader will surround themselves with people who know more than they do and they will thrive in the outstanding resource they have created. Leaders do not know everything and the sooner they realise they cannot concur the world on their own the better.

A final consideration is that the leader is still the leader as being democratic can sometimes lead to over-empowerment of staff. Although staff should be involved and have freedom the leader is still responsible for agreeing to decisions as well as creating a structured environment in which staff are able to work effectively.

Democratic leadership can be effective but it is not an easy style to master. It involves a constant balance between structure and freedom and many leaders will take years to perfect it. As with all leadership styles democratic leadership should only be used in the right situations and with the right people. It is not applicable to every situation and should be used flexibly within a more holistic leadership approach.

Task-Orientated Leadership

In any business, work is completed by people. Therefore, a leader can either focus their attention on the work being completed, the people completing the work, or both. In this case, as the name implies, task-orientated leaders are primarily concerned with the work that is being performed. They are highly goal-focused and work effectively towards predetermined objectives.

This style of leadership is less concerned with the individuals and teams performing the work just as long as the work is done on time and to the required standard. Task-orientated leaders will define the roles within a team, divide the work up amongst the team, establish processes and procedures and monitor progress. Anything and everything is focused towards achieving the task.

Almost all businesses succeed or fail as a result of their ability to produce and deliver products and services. Effective and efficient creation of products and delivery of services is crucial for businesses to succeed. A task-orientated leader will adopt a pure, direct approach to getting the job done for the greater good of the business. Products need to be made and the employees are there to make them. Services need to be delivered and the employees are there to deliver them.

Little attention is given to the attitudes, feelings, views and values of the staff. They are there to do a job and it is the purpose of the task-orientated leader to maximise their productivity. This style of leadership believes in task cohesion, whereby the achievement of goals and objectives motivates the staff to perform. A positive outcome of collectively achieving a common goal is that the staff will feel satisfied and motivated to do more.

Key Strengths

The most obvious strength for this style of leadership is that it ensures deadlines are met and tasks are completed. It can be highly effective for industries which need to meet strict deadlines while simultaneously maintaining a high standard of quality. Media publications and newspapers are a good example of this along with multiple assembly-line manufacturing. Work has to be completed by a specific time and at a specific standard and there is little room for error or delay. A task-orientated leader may be well suited to this particular type of job role.

Another key strength of task-orientated leadership is that these leaders are excellent delegators and know exactly how to divide up work and prioritise tasks to get things done. Often they will have a sound understanding of the resources required to complete a task and can be highly efficient in their planning and implementation. This can result in improved productivity as well as efficiency savings within the organisation.

As previously stated, businesses are largely measured on their level of productivity and by ensuring these levels remain high the task-orientated leader can provide growth and survival for the business as well as job security for staff. These positive outcomes provide an indirect benefit to staff even though the leader is not aiming to directly meet the needs of the staff.

Key Criticisms

A major criticism of task-orientated leadership is that it runs the risk of overlooking the welfare and happiness of the staff. Being totally focused on the task can result in the leader ignoring key issues which may arise within the team. Driving the staff to complete the task without paying attention to their personal needs can create a team which feels undervalued and unappreciated. Although there is a strong focus towards maximising productivity, task-orientated leadership can actually reduce productivity indirectly as undervalued and unappreciated employees are less likely to be motivated to maximise their performance and efforts.

Task-orientated leadership does not allow staff to be innovative, creative or spontaneous in their work. Instead they are expected to follow orders, they are given their own mini-tasks to complete and there is little scope for flexibility or adaptation. Staff working under this style of leadership can often lack enthusiasm, inspiration and the willingness to go above and beyond. With few opportunities to explore new ideas staff will typically find themselves limited in their ability to develop into more complex job roles. Progression and training is more formal in this environment which limits staff development opportunities.

With staff lacking in motivation and feeling unappreciated they are unlikely to stay within their employment for long periods of time. Although productivity may be high staff turn over will also be high which will result in additional time spent on recruiting, training and inducting new staff. This can have a detrimental impact on the whole team as the fluidity of staff turnover can affect key processes.

Final Thoughts

Within all industries there is a need for task-orientated leaders. If they didn't exist, very few tasks would every get completed. However, if all the leader does is push staff to complete tasks they run the risk of neglecting the needs of the individuals and teams performing the work. This can result in staff welfare issues as well as higher levels of demotivation.

With employees feeling undervalued and unappreciated they will be less motivated to work and in turn this will reduce productivity: the very thing task-orientated leaders are hoping to improve. Therefore, there is a clear need for task-orientated leadership to be used in combination with other contrasting leadership styles to ensure staff feel appreciated and motivated to work.

We all need to meet deadlines and for those of us who lead others we also have to make sure other people meet deadlines too. We will often find that we are subconsciously leading this way because of pressures from our own superiors, but it is important to balance this style of leadership with one which also focuses on the personal needs of the staff. This final thought brings us nicely onto the next chapter where we will be exploring relationship-orientated leadership.

Relationship-Orientated Leadership

We began the previous chapter by suggesting that a leader can either focus their attentions on the work being performed, the people performing the work, or both. In direct contrast to task-orientated leaders, relationship-orientated leaders are primarily focused on the people who perform the work. They are concerned with supporting, motivating and developing individuals and teams. They seek to establish meaningful relationships with their staff and aim to utilise this emotional connection to maximise staff performance.

Advanced levels of emotional intelligence are required for effective relationship-orientated leadership. This enables them to easily empathise with their staff and understand things from their point of view. Relationship-orientated leaders encourage effective teamwork and collaboration through enhanced relationships that exist between team members. Understanding the needs and requirements of each individual person is vital if relationship-orientated leadership is to be effective.

Relationship-orientated leaders are very personable, their 'door is always open' and they have a genuine interest in the wellbeing of their staff. People are supported and looked after in a way that enables them to perform to the best of their ability, free from distractions and emotional burden.

Relationships are developed through social cohesion within the team. By ensuring a socially united workforce the leader will be able to keep staff motivated and inspired to work. This style of leadership promotes collaboration within the team and everyone genuinely wants to see everyone else succeed and develop.

Key Strengths

By focusing on the emotional needs of the staff, relationship-orientated leaders are able to ensure they have a positive and motivated workforce. Staff will be enthused and inspired to work and will feel valued and appreciated. Although little direct focus is given to task completion, with a highly motivated team the leader can encourage higher levels of productivity.

In a well supported team of staff, personal conflicts, dissatisfaction and boredom will be minimised resulting in a happy and productive team. Free from personal issues the staff will be able to work more efficiently and at a higher standard. It is often the social and inter-personal issues that hinder performance within a team and by ensuring staff are happy, inspired and supported to work the impact of these issues can be significantly minimised.

Staff may also be more inclined to work creatively and innovatively, taking risks and challenging key operations. Staff will feel confident to take risks as they will be aware that the leader will provide support if they are unsuccessful. This is essential for development and improvements in organisational performance.

Key Criticisms

A major criticism of relationship-orientated leadership is that with a major focus on the relationships between staff the actual task being performed can sometimes be overlooked. Not wanting to work staff too hard, too much or in a way they do not enjoy, can greatly increase the risk of failure. When tight deadlines have been set and maximum effort is required, a stronger focus on the task may be needed.

Another key criticism is that some employees may take advantage of a people-focused leader. If staff see the leader accommodating their every need they may start to take liberties. Just as a child attempts to do with their parents or teacher, they will continuously push the boundaries to see what they can get away with. Once a bond has been made between the employee and the leader this is less likely to occur due to the high level of mutual respect that will have been created. However, this does not happen instantly and while the relationship is developing the leader must be mindful that the employee may try to push the limits of acceptable behaviour.

While the encouragement of risk taking is a key strength of relationship-orientated leadership it can also be considered a criticism. While risk taking is essential for the progression of an organisation the risk also needs to be calculated. Too much risk taking, at the wrong time and in the wrong place can result in irreversible errors which the leader will find difficult to repair.

Final Thoughts

Leaders have to be relationship-focused; after all, leadership is all about inspiring and motivating people to take action. If a leader does not have a clear understanding of the needs, interests and abilities of their staff, and cannot relate to them on a personal level, they will never succeed. But with this in mind it is also important for a leader to maintain focus on the task at hand. Neglecting the task in order to address the ever growing needs and demands of the staff may impact long-term success.

A balance needs to be established between meeting the needs of the staff and the needs of the task. The key is to ensure that the support provided is directly linked to the completion of the task. By doing this you enable the staff to do the best job they can and you will ensure success. We started the previous two chapters by stating that leaders can focus their attention on the work, the people doing the work, or both. The obvious answer of course, is both.

Bureaucratic Leadership

Bureaucratic leaders are highly administrative and they lead by following the rule book. Typically they do not set the rules and guidelines but rather they adhere to them. In industries where regulation and legislation have a significant impact on business operations a bureaucratic leadership style is well suited. They have a job specification to follow and they deliver on it. Never willing to stray from their chosen path spontaneity and flexibility can be counter-productive to a bureaucratic leader.

Leading in a bureaucratic style becomes particularly relevant when there is a risk of financial or legal repercussions when regulation and legislation is not addressed accurately. For some highly regulated industries with vast exposure to risk this style of leadership can be crucial for success. For example, organisations with a broad health and safety remit, or companies who have to produce products which meet a precise specification may greatly benefit from an effective bureaucratic leader.

It could be argued that this style of leadership has more in common with management than leadership as it is largely focused on the control and regulation of work. However, the bureaucratic leader will also be people-focused in their approach to leadership. By engaging, developing and empowering employees the staff will be able to work to the detailed standards and criteria that are enforced by the leader with relative autonomy. Therefore, although bureaucratic leaders ensure work is completed to the correct standards they also aim to engage their staff in the process.

Key Strengths

Through consistent routine, bureaucratic leadership ensures all staff know their roles and responsibility and are highly focused on the task at hand. This can lead to great success in task-focused work situations. Attention to detail and accountability can be very useful for an organisation, particularly if health and safety, staff welfare and precise product specifications are a priority.

When change is implemented the new processes and procedures will be tested and checked by the leader to ensure risk of failure is minimised. This precautionary approach to change can be very important in ensuring long-term success as well as minimising short-term issues and associated declines in performance.

Induction processes for new staff are very structured as clear guidelines and action points will have already been established. This not only ensures that new staff are able to work effectively and quickly but it also enables temporary staff and cover staff to fill in and perform work with clear guidelines. This can be extremely beneficial for fast-paced industries where little time is available for development and lengthy staff inductions.

Key Criticisms

One of the biggest criticisms of this style of leadership is that it does not encourage innovative and creative thinking. This can be a huge limitation for the leader as it can prevent progress and adaption within the workforce. For a business to grow and expand it must also allow its staff to do the same. This limiting leadership style can restrict this from happening which will not in the best interests of the organisation.

Staff clarity around roles and responsibilities is good however it can cause such distinct divides between staff job roles that they will be less likely to undertake work that is beyond their predetermined boundaries. This means less thinking outside the box and less collaboration with colleagues. Staff may lack the ability and scope to use their initiative and take on work outside of their remit as it may interfere with someone else's work and standards.

Staff development can be inhibited when working under a bureaucratic leader. The majority of work conducted is prescribed and instructional in nature meaning the employees are not exposed to problem solving and other higher-order thinking skills. This can limit staff potential for progression within their existing job roles and prevent upward movement of staff throughout the organisation.

Final Thoughts

There is always a case for bureaucratic leadership in every organisation. Leaders need to provide clear direction to their staff and it is essential that they meet all necessary regulatory and legal requirements. However, it is important that leaders use this style of leadership in combination with other contrasting styles as being overly bureaucratic can inhibit staff innovation and creative thinking.

As with every leadership style, it is a case of knowing when and where to use each style to maximise its impact. Staff will turn to their leader for clarity and direction, and if the proposed direction involves navigating various regulation and legislation, then the leader has to be bureaucratic. We all need to follow the rules and if the leader can provide a precise structure for staff to work within they will be sufficiently supported and guided in their pursuit of success.

Laissez Faire Leadership

'Laissez Faire' is a French term and has the literal translation of 'let it be', 'leave it alone' or 'let them do as they will'. Therefore, laissez faire leadership is all about providing complete freedom for employees to work as they see fit. This style of leadership is sometimes referred to as 'delegative' or 'hand-off' leadership due to its un-controlling nature. Staff are free to decide how they will achieve their objectives, where they will work, when they will work and who they will work with.

The freedom that laissez faire leadership provides employees is thought to motivate and enthuse staff. Netflix, the popular online video streaming company, famously announced their 'no restriction annual leave policy' whereby its employee can decide when they take their annual leave and how much they take. It is not monitored or reviewed and the only remit is that all work is completed on time and to the correct standard. If this is achieved then annual leave can be taken. Richard Branson has recently followed suit by implementing the same annual leave policy for his head office staff at Virgin.

Google is another company who have utilised this style of leadership. Whenever the public are able to get a glimpse inside their headquarters it is not uncommon to see Google staff socialising, discussing, working in bespoke clusters and generally being creative in the way they approach their jobs. Google have a commitment to staff welfare and believe this is one of the most effective ways to attract and retain the best employees.

Laissez faire leaders provide the tools and resources that are required to complete the job and then leave the staff to complete it. Staff are expected to solve problems, overcome issues and generate work plans by themselves. The leader will ensure they are available should the staff wish to consult them or provide feedback but generally speaking they will leave it up to the staff to complete the work free from interference. In some cases a laissez faire leader may even allow employees to set their own objectives providing complete freedom to work in any way they see fit.

Key Strengths

This style of leadership is extremely effective when dealing with highly motivated, knowledgeable and skilled staff whom the leader trusts. For example, if you have an experienced sales manager you may issue them with an objective and leave them to get on with the job. You believe in their ability and trust they will do a good job. In turn, they will appreciate the freedom to work independently and will feel valued and trusted by the leader.

Staff will feel empowered and take on full responsibility for their work. As they have come up with the plan and ideas themselves they will want to complete the work as they will have a personal investment in the project. Staff will see this style of leadership as a challenge and an opportunity to prove themselves to the leader. They have been trusted with a job to do and they will not want to let the leader down.

If staff members are given a complex task to complete they will find themselves testing, problem solving, evaluating, planning and collaborating with colleagues. This creates a fantastic environment for staff to grow and develop as people and employees. Generating innovative ideas through creative thinking is a common outcome of laissez faire leadership.

There is also a benefit for the leader in that they will be significantly decreasing their work load. They will spend less time managing employees, assessing, tracking, reviewing and appraising their work. As long as they trust the staff member who has been delegated the work they will be able to let go of the project and focus their attention on other areas. This enables the leader to maximise their time and increase their capacity to work.

Key Criticisms

If the leader is dealing with staff who are not highly skilled or knowledgeable this style of leadership can be disastrous. It is not to say that when dealing with poorly skilled staff laissez faire leadership cannot be used, but the objectives being set have to be suitable and achievable. Complex objectives may be too much for some staff to complete without consistent support and guidance.

It is a fact that many staff will not be very good at setting their own deadlines and targets and will be likely to leave things until the last minute. If they encounter problems they may not be equipped to deal with them effectively and if they start to lose track of the project they will only be accountable to themselves.

This style of leadership leaves the leader wide open for staff to take advantage. In order to use laissez faire leadership the leader must totally trust their staff, regardless of their skill level. They must not just trust them with regards to their efforts and commitment but also in their actual ability to complete the work to the required standard. In other words, even if an employee tries their absolute hardest, and their determination to success cannot be questioned, they may still simply not have the skills and experience to complete the work accordingly.

If the leader is not checking performance until the very end of the project, any mistakes or failures to meet deadlines may not be identified until it is too late. This can be a huge issue if the leader is expecting the work to be completed on time, to a high standard and within the allocated budget.

Final Thoughts

This is a very free and easy leadership style which can produce some highly innovative and creative work when used in the right context. But when used incorrectly the associated negative impacts can be vast. This is not a leadership style many people will be confident utilising across their entire programme but it is one that can be used in certain situations, for certain employees, on certain projects. Knowing when and with whom to use this style of leadership is the key to its success. Understanding the potential benefits and drawbacks to this style of leadership is very important for any leader who is considering using it.

It is strongly recommended that a leader begins by testing laissez faire leadership with unimportant tasks to see if the staff are up to the challenge. If they are, the leader can gradually incorporate more relevant and complex tasks over time. This is a safe way to implement this style of leadership into your practice while minimising its associated risks. By gradually introducing laisse faire leadership you will also be able to identify the employees who respond in the most positive way.

Similarly, paired work is often a good idea initially as it is difficult for people to hide when working in pairs. When working in larger groups, people can hide amongst the group with relative ease and without detection. However, if placed in pairs it is blatantly obvious if one of the two people are not pulling their weight. These are just a couple of ways you may wish to begin incorporating laissez faire leadership into your leadership armoury.

Charismatic Leadership

A charismatic leader gains followers predominantly through their engaging and charming personality as opposed to their level of power and authority. They will often be the centre of attention and will be remembered by everyone at any networking event or conference they attend. People are instantly drawn to charismatic leaders and will want to be associated with them.

When talking to people they will have the ability to make that person feel like the most important person in the world. Charismatic leaders have a great awareness of their surroundings as well as an empathy for the feelings and opinions of those they are interacting with. They are very people-focused and forge meaningful relationships with their staff.

Appearance is everything and charismatic leaders will spend a lot of time perfecting how they come across to others. People want to be around them, work for them and follow them in their endeavours wherever it may take them. They are willing to put themselves out there and take personal risk in order to pursue their ideals. Charismatic leadership can be considered as being closely aligned with the concept of 'personal branding' in that individuals lead and promote their endeavours through their own personality.

This style of leadership is very common amongst politicians and public speakers. Politicians are aware that many voters opt for the person and not necessarily the content of their manifesto. In the UK, Boris Johnson, Mayor of London, is a classic example of this. His name is actually Alexander Boris de Pfeffel Johnson but he chooses to use Boris as it is more quirky and memorable. His clown-like behaviour engages the public and for many he provides an alternative to the typical emotionless, stiff-faced politicians that people are so very fed up with. But don't be fooled, this is a very clever performance as Boris is extremely well educated and extremely astute. If I asked you who Boris Johnson is you could probably tell me – but if I asked you what he stands for I bet many people would find it rather difficult to provide a clear and concise summary of his values.

Key Strengths

Charismatic leaders are fantastic at engaging, inspiring and enthusing their staff which in turn improves the productivity and efficiency of the team. They can hold a meeting or presentation with grandeur and easily get others to agree with their vision. Their ability to hold a room and dominate situations in a non-imposing manner can result in improved negotiations and outcomes on their part.

The ability to engage others in their vision is a fundamental strength for this style of leadership. Many leaders are unable to get staff to 'buy-into' their vision and struggle to get people on-board. If employees do not support the leader's vision they will typically have an extremely difficult time leading them. A truly effective charismatic leader will have people eating out the palm of their hand and will get people to readily engage with their overall vision and purpose.

Charismatic leadership will create a highly motivated workforce which is behind the leader every step of the way. People will want to work with, work for, buy from, invest in and generally support the leader in anyway they can. What a fantastic position to be in.

individuals, groups, departments, and also the organisation as a whole, will ensure everyone within the business has the resources and tools they need to achieve their collective objectives.

Servant leadership can also have a knock-on effective on the staff exposed to it. Consider the following question, "If I serve my staff, are they more likely to become servants themselves?" It has been widely proven that people will work harder and do more to help those whom they highly trust and respect. Serve them and they will serve you back. In turn, if staff serve each other, everyone serves each other back. Everyone is empowered and everyone leads others in one way or another. If this extreme level of collaborative leadership can be achieved, the work environment will be highly productive and support throughout the entire organisation.

Key Criticisms

One of the biggest criticisms of servant leadership is the notion that no one in business should be a 'servant' or a 'slave' to anyone else. Instead they should work collaboratively with mutual support. Although it could be argued that by serving others the leader will generate mutual trust and collaboration it would be foolish to think that no one would take advantage. The majority of employees will respond positively to a servant leader but unfortunately some people will not. Abuse of this style of leadership is not uncommon with employees adopting a take, take, take-approach with very little give.

Another criticism of servant leadership is that it takes a long time to create a servant-culture within an organisation. It takes time to work with staff, facilitate their development and support them as they grow. When starting a new business the culture can be established from the onset but when attempting to implement servant leadership into an existing business, particularly one with a cemented legacy, the change in culture can take a considerable amount of time to achieve. Many leaders do not have the luxury of time and short-term gains often take priority over long-term development.

Final Thoughts

If servant leadership is implemented effectively it can be greatly beneficial to both the leader and the employees. It can be one of the most effective ways to manage and lead people as it engages them, provides support, empowers and guides. As with all other leadership styles covered within this book the use of servant leadership needs to be incorporated with other leadership styles. Some employees may naturally absorb the endless support without ever offering anything back and in such cases a different leadership style must be considered.

I don't believe servant leadership is a particularly suitable name for what it describes. Being a servant implies a one way service which is actually not how servant leadership works. It may begin that way but over time the employees who are exposed to this style of leadership will in turn serve the leader and their colleagues in a similar way, thus making it a two-way process. Servant leadership is more of a cultural leadership style and would perhaps be better termed 'servant culture'.

Regardless of these minor differences of opinion, the fundamental principles of Greenleaf's work on servant leadership has become an extremely prominent leadership style in the modern business world and one which should be incorporated into every leader's tool kit.

Summary of Leadership Styles

We have now worked through the eight leadership styles presented within this book. I hope you have found each individual style interesting and have been able to draw relevant aspects from each to help you enhance your own leadership practice. The remaining chapters in this book will aim to bring everything together by summarising the leadership styles covered. In addition, there will be a discussion on the opposing forces that exist between certain leadership style pairings. The final chapter will provide some departing thoughts and will encourage you to try out and test some of the leadership styles you have read about. We will begin here with a concise summary of the leadership styles covered within this book.

One of the key things to take away from this book is that although each individual leadership style should be considered in its own right, it is the leader's ability to adapt and utilise each style to suit the situation that will make them an effective leader. Leaders have different personalities, different job roles, different staff, different knowledge, experience and skill-sets. Therefore, it would not be right to proceed without putting this information into context and summarising how all these individual leadership styles interact and overlap.

There is no preferred leadership style

Throughout this book we have explored eight different leadership styles. I would like to make it clear that there is no single ideal leadership style that every leader should adopt. Similarly, there is no single leadership style that leaders should avoid using. Different people in different situations need to use the most appropriate leadership style to invoke the actions and outcomes that are required.

Different leadership styles should be used for different situations

Effective leaders have the ability to use different leadership styles in different situations. For example, if a member of staff is underperforming the leader may adopt a task-orientated leadership style to ensure the person has clarity and understands exactly what is expected of them. Similarly, if a leader enters a room and witnesses staff putting themselves at risk by using equipment in an inappropriate manner they may adopt an autocratic leadership style, taking control of the situation to maintain the welfare of employees. Lastly, if the leader has a team of highly experienced staff they may adopt a laissez faire style of leadership allowing freedom for completion of work. The style must match the situation.

Even within a specific situation different leadership styles could be used

This adds yet another level to the notion of there not being a single preferred leadership style. Let's look at the example used above for the underperforming staff member. A leader could approach this situation in many different ways: they could be autocratic and impose demands on the person; they could be task-orientated providing clarity; they could be relationship-orientated to gain a better understanding of the underlying issues; or they could adopt the approach of servant leader supporting the staff member to achieve their objectives. All of these examples could be effective and the success of the style the leader adopts will be largely dependent on their personality, experience and the nature of the staff member being dealt with.

The leadership style is sometimes dictated by the nature of the job role

Certain leadership styles are frequently observed in different business sectors. For example, head chefs are typically seen barking autocratic orders at their staff in this deadline-ridden environment. Similarly, when it is literally a matter of life or death, military leaders will traditionally adopt an autocratic approach to leadership. However, take the example of Google where the majority of staff are highly skilled and highly motivated. At Google most staff follow a laissez faire leadership style where they have the freedom to work where they want, when they want and with whom they want. There are obviously exceptions to the rule but it appears that some leadership styles naturally align themselves with specific business sectors more than others and staff within these sectors seems to respond better to certain leadership styles.

Understanding the different leadership styles is essential

The majority of leaders with find themselves in a business sector that does not overly align with one particular leadership style. In this environment the leader will find themselves constantly jumping from one style to another as they address the ever changing obstacles of a 'typical' workday. If a leader has a sound understanding of the different leadership styles that are available they will be in a better position to offer appropriate leadership to suit every situation. Knowing when and how to be supportive, instructional, caring, task focused and charismatic can greatly enhance a leader's overall effectiveness.

Where possible leaders should work to their strengths

The natural personality and past experiences of the leader will have a significant impact on their preferred leadership styles. If you are fortunate enough to be born with bundles of confidence and charisma, charismatic leadership will come naturally to you. Similarly, if you are a caring and supportive person it may feel more natural adopting a relationship-orientated approach to leadership. Good leaders work to their strengths but also work hard to develop the areas that do not come quite so naturally to them. Extending on from the previous point, it is essential to understand the different leadership styles that are available, but it is also essential to know what you do best and what you need to work on.

Opposing Relationships Between Leadership Styles

As you have progressed through this book you may have started to identify some opposing differences between some of the leadership styles covered. This chapter aims to highlight these contrasting pairings and further explore the relationships that exist. Each of the opposing leadership style pairs can be considered on a continuum whereby the leader moves flexibly from one position to another in relation to the situations that are presented.

Autocratic v Democratic

Autocratic leadership is instructional in nature whereas democratic leadership in inclusive of staff opinion. Effective leaders have the ability to move along this scale utilising each style as the situation requires. At one end the leader can be autocratic and controlling in their approach to leadership and at the other end the leader can be democratic and engaging.

Task-Orientated v Relationship-Orientated

Leaders are either concerned with the task being completed or concerned with the relationships among the people who are completing the task. There is no right or wrong here but rather a fine balance needs to be maintained between ensuring the safety and happiness of the individuals and teams performing the work as well as ensuring the task is completed in the timeframe required. It is a difficult task but effective leaders are able to maintain this balance at all times.

Bureaucratic v Laissez Faire

Bureaucratic leaders lead by the book and provide clear direction to their staff which must be adhered to. Opposing this style is laissez faire which allows staff to work freely in an unrestricted manner. There is a need for both leadership styles and outstanding leaders understand when to tighten and loosen the autonomy-chains to suit the person and situation involved.

Charismatic v Servant

These two leadership style are less in opposition than the previous three examples but they do conflict each other in one fundamental way. Charismatic leaders are very intrinsically focused whereas servant leaders are very extrinsically focused. Charismatic leaders are largely concerned with people following them and 'getting on-board' with their vision. Servant leaders are more staff-focused and are concerned with supporting others to become the best they can be. Leading with charisma and serving others can work hand-in-hand but effective leaders are aware of the differences between the two and know when and how to use each to maximise impact.

Additional Leadership Style Theories

In this penultimate chapter we will be exploring some additional leadership style theories to ensure you have a broader understanding of the subject. Throughout the core of this book I chose to specifically focus on eight distinct leadership styles. This is because I believe they provide a comprehensive overview of the topic and more than adequately cover the fundamental elements of leadership styles. However, there are a number of other leadership theories, concepts and styles which are also relevant. In most cases they incorporate many of the styles we have already covered but the way in which they categorise and emphasise different leadership styles will further our exploration of this topic. It is also important that you gain a broader understand of leadership theory as the concepts included within this chapter are commonly referenced in discussions.

Tannenbaum and Schmidt's Leadership Continuum

Robert Tannenbaum and Warren Schmidt devised a leadership style continuum in the 1950s consisting of seven stages. Each stage of the continuum involves a gradual reduction in the use of managerial powers which coincides with a gradual increase in employee freedom. The seven stages are outlined below:

1. Leader makes decisions and announces them
2. Leader "sells" decisions
3. Leader presents ideas and invites questions
4. Leader presents tentative decisions which are subject to change
5. Leader presents problems, gets suggestions and makes

decisions

6. Leader defines limits and asks the group to make decisions

7. Leader permits employees to function within the limits defined

If we are to reflect back on the eight leadership styles covered earlier in this book it is possible to align some with this continuum. For example, stage 1: Leader makes decisions and announces them; can be aligned with autocratic leadership and stage 7: Leader permits employees to function within the limits defined; can be aligned to democratic leadership. However, not all leadership styles covered are easily aligned to this continuum.

The continuum is more concerned with power and empowerment as opposed to task and relationship orientation. In addition, there is little attention paid to charismatic and bureaucratic leadership styles. When considering power, authority and engagement Tannenbaum and Schmidt's leadership continuum provides a relevant model but when exploring leadership styles in a broader context this model is found lacking.

McGregor's X and Y Theory

The X and Y theory was proposed by Douglas McGregor in 1960 and it provides a similar concept to that of Tannenbaum and Schmidt. McGregor observed a number of leaders and managers operating in their place of work and as a result he concluded that every leader could be categorised as either an 'X leader' or a 'Y leader'.

Theory X proposes that humans have an inherent dislike for work and will avoid it where possible. Similarly, most people prefer to be directed, try to avoid responsibility, have little ambition and are happy with security alone. An 'X Leader' will attempt to counter this dislike by controlling, directing, coercing, threatening and punishing employees in order to get them to work. This is a very autocratic and task-orientated approach to leadership and follows a 'control and command' style.

Theory Y proposes that humans have a natural desire to work and pursue challenging goals. If the situation is favourable people will find work to be a source of satisfaction, fulfilment and enjoyment. When trusted and engaged people have the ability to work productively and effectively in a self-controlled and self-directed manner. This is a highly democratic or even servant style of leadership and follows an 'engage and enthuse' style.

McGregor's X and Y theory provides a good starting point for leadership style exploration however, as with Tannenbaum and Schmidt's leadership continuum, the X and Y theory is fairly limited to autocratic and democratic leadership styles and neglects other important factors.

Situational Leadership

Paul Hersey and Ken Blanchard evolved previous work by Bill Reddin and proposed the concept of situational leadership. This theory suggests that different situations require different leadership styles. Leaders must have the ability to adapt and adjust their style in order to suit the context and requirements of the situation they are presented with. Situational leadership outlines four predominant leadership styles: directing, coaching, supporting and delegating.

There are many similarities between these four styles and the ones previously covered in this book. Directing, coaching, supporting and delegating are ultimately nothing more than variations in terminology. The previous two chapters have also discussed the need for adapting leadership styles to meet the needs of the situation. Although we have previously covered the key concepts and ideas behind situational leadership it is still important to include and present this theory within this chapter. By emphasising the importance of situational factors in relation to adopting leadership styles, situational leadership provided a key turning point in the development of leadership theory.

Action-Centred Leadership

Another situational approach to leadership was proposed by John Adair in 1973 which he named, 'Action-Centred Leadership'. Adair's model is more of an approach to leadership than a style however as it incorporates three fundamental leadership styles within the model it has been included in this chapter.

Action-centred leadership suggests that a leader must apply equal levels of concern for the task being completed, the team performing the task and the individuals within the team. By consistently focusing on task, team and individuals the leader will ensure all important factors are addressed. However, there is also scope for the leader to place emphasis on one or two particular areas as and when the situation requires. This is therefore an adaptable model which can be modified to meet the requirements of the situation.

Transactional Leadership

This style of leadership was highly popular throughout the 1970s and 1980s. It involves meaningful exchanges between the leader and employees in order to meet the interests of both parties. Employees work towards the achievement of specific organisational objectives in exchange for rewards and recognition, both financially and non-financially. Effective transactional leadership should incorporate contingent reward and management of expectations.

Reward should be provided to motivate employees to work productively such as bonuses, praise and recognition. Expectations need to be managed effectively through constructive criticism and feedback channels in order to correct errors and promote development over the long-term. Transactional leaders are much more focused on the 'now' and are concerned with day-to-day operations and objectives. Often they will lack the ability to see the bigger picture and create visions for the future.

Transformational Leadership

The concept of transformational leadership began in the late 1970s and it has had a large impact on the way modern leaders think and behave. It involves the leader engaging, supporting and empowering their employees. Transformational leaders are often highly charismatic and work to serve and include their employees in the work they perform. Employees want to be inspired, enthused and motivated to work and transformational leaders aim to make this a reality.

Warren Bennis and Burt Nanus have outlined what they believe to be the essential qualities of an effective transformational leader.

1. Having a clear vision for the future
2. Being a 'social architect' for their organisation
3. Creating trust through consistency and clarity
4. Having positive self-regard

To summarise, transformational leaders are considered as having a clear vision, highly levels of emotional intelligence, bundles of charisma and exemplary standards of consistency and integrity demonstrated in their behaviour.

Responsible Leadership

Within the modern business world it is essential that leaders are authentic and responsible. They need to be genuine, honest and trustworthy in their actions at all times. The concept of responsible or authentic leadership has evolved out of a response to the expressed need of key stakeholders who wish to be associated with responsible businesses and responsible leaders. Investors, customers, employees, suppliers and local communities want to invest in, buy from, work for and be associated with businesses who are responsible in their operations.

Responsible leadership involves the leader actively demonstrating the values of the business in tandem with their own personal values. This promotes integrity and authenticity in their behaviour. This is more of an ethos towards leadership as opposed to a distinct leadership style in its own right, however it is a great place to end this chapter as the ethos of responsible leadership should underpin the use of any other leadership style covered within this book. Regardless of whether a leader is being autocratic, democratic, charismatic or bureaucratic they need to ensure they are being authentic and responsible in their actions at all times.

We began this book by explaining that a leadership style if nothing more than a style and that the fundamental principles of leadership must be present at all times in order to be effective. These fundamental principles are summed up within the concepts of responsible and authentic leadership.

Departing Thoughts

I sincerely hope you have found this book on leadership style both interesting and enjoyable. I also hope you have been able to extract some relevant points of interest to use in your own leadership practice. This final short chapter will outline some considerations to think about with regard to implementing leadership styles.

Like many professions, leadership is all about acquiring as many tools and skills as you can and using them in the most effective way possible. As a sports coach you would have a play-book or a series of tactical moves that you could use. Understanding what you 'could' do is okay, but to be successful you need to know what you 'should' do. Therefore, reading this book and gaining an understanding of the different leadership styles that are available for use is great, but in order to be an effective leader you will need to understand how and when to use them.

Unfortunately, this cannot be taught in a straight forward fashion due to the differences that exist within every business, department, team and individual. Therefore, it is up to the leader to utilise the tools that are at their disposal and select the best play form their play-book to address the situation or issue that presents itself.

As a leader within an organisation you will be constantly moving back and forth along all four of the opposing spectrums. You will have to be autocratic to maintain staff welfare and then instantly democratic during meetings; task-orientated to meet a tight deadline and then relationship-focused to deal with a staff grievance; bureaucratic to adhere to legal regulations while allowing freedom for your staff to work innovatively (laissez faire); and charismatic to deliver a sales presentation as well as servant to ensure your staff have the resources they need to succeed.

Leadership is a very complex skill to implement effectively. All of these changes between leadership styles will often happen on a subconscious level and will be instigated through your prior knowledge and experience. Consciously trying and testing different leadership styles in different situations can be a great way to challenge yourself professionally and also to assess what works and what does not. It allows you to establish which styles come most naturally to you and also which styles your staff respond to best as individuals and teams.

Made in United States
North Haven, CT
09 October 2022

25099818R00033